This book is a must-read for every parent with a child who has struggled in life. It is laced with the Word of God and contains His promises laid out straight from the Bible. Every day ther _____ _____'s prayer followed by a decree stated in language based on _____ prayed.

Because You Prayed is a power-p_ _____ that bring hope, strength, and healin_ _____ I have seen many men enter our faith _____ because of the power of a praying m _____ the grace of God bring salvation and transformation. A v_____ _____, process has certainly been that 'prayer power' of the hopeful mom. It has been such a joy to see them returned to their families to live the lives that God had intended.

—**Randy Makinson**
Spiritual Formation Coach
Teen Challenge Men's Center, Lanigan, SK
www.teenchallenge.ca

It has been a privilege to walk with Judy Mizu as editor of her book *Because You Prayed*. I had a close-up view of what she wrote during her journey praying for her son. I found myself going down into the deep crevices of near-despair with this mother. Then, buoyed by the Word of the Lord, which she had grabbed as her lifeline, I would emerge with restored confidence and renewed expectation.

To say that Judy's journey is "authentic" is an understatement! She does not mask nor minimize her own need for the Lord's fresh deposit of forgiveness, strength, or patience.

More than once, I would note back to the author that "there's someone waiting to read that line." Now "someone" holds this book in his or her hand. Even if yours is a white-knuckle grip, allow the substance and momentum to flow to you. This book is your invitation to dip into that same divine deposit that this family discovered as you read the journey of their "heart-fought" victory.

—**Peggy Kennedy**
Speaker and Author
A is for Apple, Hear the Sound, Chosen
www.TwoSilverTrumpets.ca

Whatever the present state of your life and family, if you believe there is potential for something greater, and there certainly is, then it is time to go to war. Judy shares her claim to victory and the day-to-day commitment required to get you there. Faith sees a better future, and action leads to victory!

—Al Purvis, Asian Director
World Mission Continuum Society
www.victoryasia.com

I have known Judy since 2005. I met her at a Teen Challenge graduation where her son, Justin, successfully graduated from the twelve-month rehabilitation program. I was so impressed with Justin; but, when I looked at Judy, I could tell she had been through a war. After I read this book, I understood what she had been through. Her prayers and declarations saved her son's life. And I thank God for that because today, Justin is my son-in-law, and an amazing worship leader in our church. This is a profound yet practical book. It is a great tool for those who are battling for their children's lives.

—Terry Severson, Pastor
Christ the Healer Gospel Church
www.christthehealer.net

The reason for the victorious power that Jesus displayed on earth was that He was in partnership with His Father. Judy also has a partnership with heaven and experienced this same authority over her circumstances and victory in answered prayer. Hers is the testimony of a mother who wrapped herself in prayer and faith. Believing what God says, she overcame the challenges of the physical realm by tapping into the supernatural.

Overcoming gives us power in the Kingdom of God. A warrior emerges to believe for the miraculous!!! As you walk through Judy's journey, you will see her merging warrior heart in action. This author can affirm that Jeremiah 1:12 can become our experience! God, Himself watches over His Word to perform it—to make sure it comes to pass. This book can enhance daily prayer and decrees. I would recommend it as a tool for prayer.

—Shell Rogers, **National Prayer Coordinator**
Aglow International Canada

I had known Judy and her family from before Justin was born. I reconnected with her during the time of Justin's dark struggle. I had the challenge and privilege of walking with them through the darkness as God brought Justin into His marvellous light.

That journey was definitely a process. Day twenty of this resourceful book illustrates that. Recorded there is Judy's prayer, *"Stir to my child's remembrance the teachings from Your Word and the goodness they offer. May they have more attraction than the ways of the world that lead to destruction and death."* I remember at one point Justin saying, "I want to want Jesus like or more than I want these drugs." The link back to his mother's prayer is obvious.

This book of prayers will turn your heart in faith to the God who is better and brighter than anything this world could offer. He is more powerful than the deepest darkest addiction. Thank you, Judy, for sharing your faith journey through these prayers and declarations of faith.

—**Dallas Block, Executive Director**
Rock Solid Refuge Inc.
www.rocksolidrefuge.com

JUDY MIZU

Because You
Prayed

Heart Cries for the
Destiny of a Loved One

BECAUSE YOU PRAYED...
HEART CRIES FOR THE DESTINY OF A LOVED ONE
Copyright © 2022 by Judy Mizu

Unless otherwise indicated, Scripture quotations are taken from The Holy Bible, New International Version® NIV® Copyright © 1973 1978 1984 2011 by Biblica, Inc. TM Used by permission. All rights reserved worldwide. • Scripture quotations marked AMP are taken from the Amplified Bible, Copyright © 1954, 1958, 1962, 1964, 1965, 1987 by the Lockman Foundation. Used by permission. • Scripture quotations marked ESV are taken from The Holy Bible, English Standard Version, Copyright © 2001 by Crossway, a publishing ministry of Good News Publishers. Used by permission. All rights reserved. • Scripture quotations marked NKJV are taken from the New King James Version®. Copyright © 1982 by Thomas Nelson. Used by permission. All rights reserved. • Scripture marked NLT are taken from the Holy Bible, New Living Translation, Copyright © 1996, 2004, 2007 by Tyndale House Foundation. Used by permission of Tyndale House Publishers, Inc., Carol Stream, Illinois 60188. All rights reserved.

ISBN: 978-1-4866-2239-9
eBook ISBN: 978-1-4866-2240-5

Word Alive Press
119 De Baets Street Winnipeg, MB R2J 3R9
www.wordalivepress.ca

WORD ALIVE
—P R E S S—

Cataloguing in Publication information can be obtained from Library and Archives Canada.

DEDICATION

I DEDICATE THIS BOOK TO my grandchildren Oscar, Lydia, and Henry, who bring this Grandma so much joy and always bring to remembrance the goodness of God.

Now to him who is able to do immeasurably more than all we ask or imagine, according to his power that is at work within us, to him be glory in the church and in Christ Jesus throughout all generations, for ever and ever! Amen.
(Ephesians 3:20-21)

CONTENTS

Part Two

A Letter from My Son

ACKNOWLEDGEMENTS

FIRST AND FOREMOST, I THANK God for His faithfulness throughout my life. I also want to acknowledge and thank everyone who came alongside my family and me and prayed for us through our journey.

For the writing of this book, I wish to thank the following by name: I thank Carter Johnson, who specifically prayed for me to write this book as an encouragement to others. I thank Darlene Polachic for her guidance in the beginning stages. I thank Peggy Kennedy for her heavenly insights and ongoing encouragement as an overall editor and project manager. To Grace, Lin, Pauline, Fern, Melody, and Linda, I thank you guys for your input, inspiration, and prayers. I thank my family for their constant love, support, and prayers. I lovingly thank my son, Justin Mizu, who graciously wrote the letter to me for this book, and who lives out his own faith, greatly inspiring and encouraging me and others.

FOREWORD

I AM A DAILY DEVOTIONAL book reader. There are numerous such books to choose from. This one is unique and written by a mother whose son became a prodigal. Judy raised her son as a single parent in a strong faith environment. Despite having the best church and spiritual activities as a youth, her son went astray deep into addiction. Judy's only hope was in God through prayer.

She never hid her son's addiction but solicited the prayers of friends and family members. These devotional writings were birthed during this mother's fight of faith on behalf of her son's journey from darkness to light in Christ.

I have seen hundreds of redemption stories like Justin's, but it is rare to read from a mother's heart how God answered her prayers for her son. I highly recommend this book. For anyone who has faced the challenges of a loved one with major bondage in their life, these daily devotions offer reasons for hope. Addiction does not need to be a life sentence, but for Justin and his mother, it was a life lesson.

—Don Wilkerson
Co-Founder
Teen Challenge Inc.

INTRODUCTION

I AM THE MOTHER OF a son who had an addiction to crystal meth-amphetamine, which began in his teen years and continued into early adulthood. Our lives became full of turmoil, with the addiction almost taking his life numerous times. It did not look like there was any hope; but, by God's life-changing power, he was set free and ignited with a passion and joy of the Lord to live out his true destiny.

I believe the blueprint for God's giftings and God's plans and purposes for children are written on the hearts of mothers. A mother's heart for her child is tender but so full of love and hope for them. I believe God had a plan for my son from the beginning of time. Even before he was born, God wrote that plan on my heart. Although, during his struggles, I questioned God as to what was happening and why. By His grace, I never lost sight of these plans that God had shown me, even during the chaos, the heartache, and the pain.

God's plans for my son included *my* part as a mother—to pray and *contend* for his destiny despite what we were seeing and experiencing as a family. How God carried through on His plans far exceeded what I had asked, thought, or imagined. To this day, God continues to do abundantly beyond what I ask, think, or imagine in the life of my son and our family.

I raised my son as a single parent. We had a strong bond with each other, with family, with God, and with the church. My son was involved in the church in many areas: Sunday School, Youth Group, Bible Quizzing, and drumming on a worship team. He was also in a Christian band that travelled and played for various events. When he turned sixteen, I marvelled at how well he was doing and how bright his future was ahead of him. We had been on a short-term mission trip together and started planning a longer-term trip for the following year. Things weren't perfect as we did have some struggles, but we had been getting through them together, and we had a close relationship. Seven months later, this *all* seemed to change in a blink of an eye. I did not understand it, and I had so many questions: What happened? How did it happen? I was frantically searching for answers.

The changes seemed to happen overnight. Before my very eyes, I saw my cheerful and happy son become angry and pull away from his close relationships, including me. He withdrew from everything. I hadn't dealt with any of these things before and never thought I would have to. My questions continued: What should I do? What could I do?

When I *did* do something, it seemed like things got worse. When I *did not* do anything, things got worse. Nothing I did or did not do seemed to make any difference. I found out that he was using drugs. This quickly became an addiction. And then... not much later, I discovered that he was using crystal methamphetamine. His health was deteriorating. His emotions were erratic.

I came to the point where I began to see that the only One who could do something was God. I had to trust Him and His Word, lean on Him and allow Him to carry me when I did not have the strength. I was learning "skilled dependency" while determining to do my best as a mother. Although I saw glimpses of God at work in miraculous ways, things continued to worsen. Yes, I made mistakes along the way, but God worked in the midst of them. I learned that God loved my son more than I did, and I could entrust my son to Him.

I realized that there were a lot of people who cared. So many people prayed and encouraged me. I cannot even begin to name them all. They included family members, friends, ministries, community members, people we were connected to, and people who were connected to the people we were connected to—and their prayer groups! Each one was vital in bringing forth the saving, healing, and restoration grace from God to my son. I am so thankful for them.

Through the time of my son's struggles, I was desperate. During our family's pain, confusion, and heartache, I prayed and cried out to God. I was driven to time with God in prayer and in reading the Bible. God so faithfully placed verses upon my heart to hold onto. These verses served as anchors of strength, especially when I needed my hope restored. As I read the Bible or prayed, God gave me timely scriptures to pray for my son. The Spirit would often generate prayer through me based on the passages I read.

I kept notes in a journal and wrote down the scriptures and my prayers. Now, throughout this book, *Because You Prayed,* I have included scriptures and prayers from that journal in the hope that it will help you as it did me. My prayer is that you will find refreshed confidence in the Lord and receive His strength and stamina for your journey as declared in Isaiah 40:31:

> *"... but those who hope in the Lord will renew their strength. They will soar on wings like eagles; they will run and not grow weary, they will walk and not be faint."*

I encourage you to open your heart while reading the passages from the Bible as found throughout these days of prayer. Allow God's Spirit to strengthen you by his Word and bring you wisdom and revelation. I am confident He will (Jeremiah 1:12)!

(Please note that all scripture verses are in the New International Version (NIV) unless otherwise stated. All pronouns for our children are in the masculine form for convenience. If you want to pray the prayers in this book, please feel free to use the appropriate "he or she" pronoun for your child.)

Part One

Thirty Days of Prayer

Day One

THE LORD IS MY STRENGTH

The Lord is my strength and my shield; my heart trusts in him, and he helps me. My heart leaps for joy, and with my song I praise him. (Psalm 28:7)

MY PRAYER

FATHER, TODAY I COME TO You needing You in my weakness. I have so many questions and concerns for my child. I feel overwhelmed. I reach to You, Lord, for your Word reminds me that You give strength. And that indeed, You *are* strength. Help me to exchange my weakness for your strength daily. Remove the veil from my eyes, Lord, to see You at work on behalf of my child.

Remind me that You are faithfully shielding and protecting us from harm and the enemy's attacks. Forgive me for not having confidence in You that You are active in guarding us against these destructive forces. Forgive me for accusing You of leaving us unguarded. Anchor me by these reminders when I am nearly swamped by the swirling thoughts that confound me concerning my child.

In the moments when the enemy's aggressive advance in my child's life or in mine seems unstoppable, raise up Your promised shield. Increase my capacity to trust in You for Your help. Take me past all the fearful dread and anxiety. Release instead a song of joy in my conflicted heart.

In Jesus's name, amen.

DECREE

The Lord is my help, my strength, and my shield. The Lord strengthens my heart by His Word, His presence, and His power. I will trust the Lord to help me. He is my portion forever. When I am weak, then I am strong because of the Lord who gives me strength. Help is here now, and help is also on the way!

Psalm 73:26; Philippians 4:13; Isaiah 40:29

Day Two

GOD IS DEPENDABLE

Jesus gave them this answer: "Very truly I tell you, the Son can do nothing by himself, he can do only what he sees his Father doing, because whatever the Father does, the Son also does. For the Father loves the Son and shows him all he does. Yes, and he will show him even greater works than these, so that you will be amazed." (John 5:19-20)

MY PRAYER

DEAR GOD, AS I READ and reflect on these truths from Your Word, I come depending upon You. I lay down my knowledge. I set aside my pride in parenting and the feeling that I know *how* to help make things better. Truthfully, I do not know what to do, and I need You. I lay these two areas at Your feet: my knowledge and my pride. I surrender them there so that they can die.

I exchange them instead for Your resurrected ways that bring life. I confess that in the surrender, I become unsure and even fearful as I relinquish control. Teach me, God, to be dependent on You and to know and understand Your will. Help me to break *free* so that Your Spirit can *break forth* and expand in *all* areas of my life, even as You work in the life of my loved one.

Father, there are times I feel paralyzed under the weight of need in our family. I pray that *by Your Spirit,* You would mobilize me according to Your thoughts and Your direction. When You have done this, then together we can go forth in Your power and Your might. Help me, Jesus, to live this out in my life today.

In Jesus's name, amen.

DECREE

Father, today I choose to participate in what You, Jesus, and the Holy Spirit are doing. Your resurrected ways always bring life! Your thoughts mobilize me in Your redemptive directions. Let Your will be done on earth as it is in heaven. Then we will be shown even greater works by You, and we will be amazed!

Galatians 2:20; John 6:35-40; John 4:16

Day Three

GOD IS MY PRINCE OF PEACE

*Do not be anxious about anything, but in every
situation, by prayer and petition, with thanksgiving,
present your requests to God. And the peace of
God, which transcends all understanding
will guard your hearts and your minds
in Christ Jesus. (Philippians 4:6-7)*

MY PRAYER

LORD, I COME BEFORE YOU today in surrender to the authority of
Christ. I yield to You and allow You, the Prince of Peace, to govern
my life. How amazing that while You are my Saviour and my tender
Shepherd, You are also pictured in the Word as a military leader
who is setting the guard around my heart and mind.

Because of *Who* You are, I choose to let go of all my *"why"*
questions. Instead, I will trust you, sovereign God, and allow Your
peace to wash over me like summer rain. I have lived in the atmosphere of frustrated effort and disappointment until my faith has
worn thin. How many times, Lord, have I come to You and others
for answers. I have seen You work miracles and bring helpers. For
that, I am very thankful and in awe of You. Yet, at times, things have

taken a turn for the worse. I am at the end of myself and choose to turn to You.

Today, I choose to surrender to Your sovereignty. You are worthy of my trust. Your peace will be my refreshing. Lord, I place my child in Your hands and believe You will take care of him.

In Jesus's name, amen.

DECREE

Today, I choose You to govern my life. I reject the options that are demanding attention from my flesh, and I choose peace. You, Yourself are my peace. I walk in the assurance that You will never leave me nor forsake me. Because You are faithful, so are Your promises to me. I embrace them to set the atmosphere of peace. You are totally sufficient today for my situation as Wonderful Counsellor, Mighty God, Everlasting Father, and yes, *Prince of Peace!* I am in relationship with a God who is true to His Name and to His Word. Today, I will live in grace, mercy, and peace as my confidence.

Ephesians 2:14; Deuteronomy 31:6; Isaiah 9:6;
2 John 1:3; John 14:27

Day Four

GOD GIVES PURPOSE

The Lord will fulfill His purpose for me; your
steadfast love, O Lord, endures forever.
Do not forsake the work of your hands.
(Psalms 138:8, ESV)

MY PRAYER

THANK YOU, FATHER, THAT YOU are at work in me even as I bring my child before You. Although I still have constant questions about what is happening, I find myself looking to You for Your higher purpose in this season. Father, reveal Your will to me for this day. Strengthen me to do it. The enemy has worked overtime to derail the destiny of my beloved child and our family. Despite the pain and disappointment of seeing the activity of the opposer, I remain confident that we are not forsaken.

My greatest concern will always be the eternal salvation of my child. However, I also contend for the destiny You have placed upon his life. I am thankful for Your promise that You will fulfill Your purpose for my child and me. Through the years, and even before my child was born, I had glimpses of that destiny. Yet, there is so much more than even I, as a parent, could desire. So many times,

I have been tempted to think that I will never see that divine plan. But Your love is steadfast and enduring—even when mine runs out. Thank you that You ordained all our days, and they were written in Your book before any of them came to be. I rest in the assurance of Your plans, purposes, and Your love for us.

In Jesus's name, amen.

DECREE

The Lord will fulfill His purpose for my child and me. Each step we take will bring us closer to our destiny. I am certain that God is working in us to will and to act in order to fulfill His good purpose. All our days were ordained and written by His hand before one of them came to be. The Lord directs our steps to fulfill our purpose.

Philippians 2:13; Psalm 139:16; Proverbs 20:24

Day Five

KNOWING GOD

*I will give them a heart to know me, that I am the
Lord. They will be my people, and I will be their
God, for they will return to me with
all their heart.* (Jeremiah 24:7)

*"No longer will they teach their neighbor,
or say to one another, 'Know the Lord,'
because they will all know me, from the least
of them to the greatest," declares the Lord. "For
I will forgive their wickedness and will remember
their sins no more."* (Jeremiah 31:34)

MY PRAYER

FATHER, THANK YOU FOR YOUR pronouncements in these verses
spoken by Your Spirit through the prophetic Jeremiah. I thank You
over and over again for Your Word that reveals Your heart for Your
people. Reveal Your heart afresh for my child and me. Help me to
remain confident that You are loving and forgiving. Show me afresh,
O Lord, that rather than discarding Your children in our tendency to
sin, You love us and desire that we know You.

I ask that in Your love and by Your power, you will give my child a heart to know You, Lord. Guide him to return to You. Father, in Your mercy work, so my child will seek Your forgiveness. Restore to him the wonder that he can be forgiven, and his sins would be remembered no more. Give him singleness of heart and action, so he will always fear You for his own good and for the good of his children after him. Inspire him to fear You, so he will never turn away from You.

I thank You, Lord, that even today, You are stirring this in my child's heart. While You are at work in his inner life, I give You fresh permission to work in mine.

In Jesus's name, amen.

DECREE

With God's help, my child will be given a heart to know the Lord. He will return to God with all his heart. He will grow in the grace and knowledge of Jesus as Lord and Savior. He will know the love of Christ that surpasses knowledge and be filled with the fullness of God. It will go well for our family. He will be a firm planting of the Lord.

2 Peter 3:17-18; Ephesians 3:19; Jeremiah 32:39; Isaiah 61:3

Day Six

GOD IS TRUSTWORTHY

You will keep in perfect peace those whose minds
are steadfast, because they trust in you.
(Isaiah 26:3)

When I am afraid, I put my trust in you.
(Psalm 56:3)

MY PRAYER

FATHER, I AM FEELING FEARFUL as I face so many things that are out of my control or influence with my child today. Help me to wait, to stand back, and to let go rather than insist on my own strength and wisdom. Lord, help me to trust and allow You to take the lead. Help me to receive Your assurance that things will turn out for good. Help me to realize that I have no peace when I look only at the present circumstances.

Provide fresh confirmation from Your promises to help me. Bring Your peace to displace the constant onslaught against my mind. I reach toward You today. Give me fresh grace to learn to trust in You continually. When I trust You, Father, I do not need to be afraid. How different is the level of peace that I experience when I choose to keep my mind stayed on You? Anchor my swirling thoughts back into what You have already revealed to me!

Thank You, Father, that You understand my fears and do not reject me because of them. Empower me to hold fast to You when I stand in faith. In that position, fear is never my desired option. Forgive me for any and all accusations that You are less than a trustworthy Father. I now choose to entrust You with my child.

In Jesus's name, amen.

DECREE

I will trust and not be afraid. I will keep my mind steadfast on the Lord. I will not fear for myself, my child, nor for my family. The Lord is trustworthy even when I do not understand. I will stand in my faith in God and His Word. As I trust in Him, He keeps my mind in perfect peace.

Proverbs 35:6; Isaiah 12:2; Psalm 143:8

Day Seven

GOD IS MY REFUGE

Have mercy on me, my God, have mercy on me,
for in you I take refuge. I will take refuge in the
shadow of your wings until the disaster
has passed. (Psalm 57:1)

MY PRAYER

LORD, MUCH HAS HAPPENED THAT I did not expect or imagine. Each day, many new disasters are rising. Although there are times of reprieve, another disaster soon comes along. There's so much happening that is unexpected—but I know it is not unexpected for You. Amid many uncertainties, of this I am certain: I am confident of Your mission and purpose for my child and me. When I face these disasters, I will take refuge in the shadow of Your wings until it has passed. Thank You for Your mercy on my child and me.

You are my child's Protector. Please keep him safe and under Your wings of protection. When I am not with my child, I know You are with him. Help him to walk a straight path with You. Open his heart and mind to recognize that You are his refuge. Cause him to run to You and not from You. Thank You that You send forth Your love and mercy to my family and me.

Lord, I take comfort in You, for You are a place of safety and assurance. Thank You for Your Word that reminds me that You are aware of my situation and my child's situation. As You hear our cries, shelter us. We are safe in You, our faithful God.

In Jesus's name, amen.

DECREE

The Lord is my refuge. I am safe underneath the shadow of His wings and in His everlasting arms. Each day, the Lord faithfully expresses his mercy, and we are not consumed. The Lord is an ever-present help in trouble. I will not fear. I will be comforted. The Lord is my child's Protector. He will keep him safe and under His protection.

Psalm 36:7-8; Lamentations 3:22-23; Deuteronomy 33:27; Psalm 46:1-2

Day Eight

GOD IS THE MERCIFUL HEALER

I have seen their ways, but I will heal them; I will
guide them and restore comfort to
Israel's mourners, creating praise
on their lips. (Isaiah 57:18-19)

MY PRAYER

DEAR GOD, I THANK YOU again for Your Word that gives insight
to Your heart and Your power. As I read Your Word, help me to
recognize Your merciful promise for my child: a promise that You
have seen his ways, but You will heal him. For far too long, the
enemy has been tormenting him and trapping him in lies. He has
now become enslaved to substances and sin beyond his ability to
break free on his own. This enslavement is affecting his mind, his
emotions, and his body. Help me, Lord, to hang on to Your promise
that things can be different. You know my frustration as his needs
now far exceed what I can do to guide or lead him to freedom. He
needs You, Lord. He needs Your healing. I ask You, Lord, in Your
mercy, release him from this bondage. Cut through every chain,
and bring supernatural intervention to heal him.

Lord, our family urgently needs You to guide and lead us. When
I am closed in behind the mountain of misery, show me again that

You go before us and will remain beside us. Although sinful actions have created so much risk, I call upon You to guard us in Your mercy.

I marvel when I am reminded of all that You are in both Your might and Your mercy. Even before the breakthrough comes, I will praise You in advance, that You are a healer, a comforter, and a trusted guardian. I thank You that You will continue to be all these things (and more) to both my child and me. These truths remind me that we both need a saviour. We both need You.

In Jesus's name, amen.

DECREE

The Lord is merciful. He loves my child in his present state. He will heal my child, rescuing him from the grave. He will heal his backsliding, guiding him towards his true destiny. In God's mercy, He will restore comfort to my child and me. God is good, and His mercy endures forever.

Isaiah 66:13; Hosea 14:4 Psalm 136:1 (NKJV)

Day Nine

GOD IS MY CHILD'S TEACHER

*All your children will be taught by the Lord, and
great will be their peace.* (Isaiah 54:13)

MY PRAYER

DEAR FATHER, AS I READ the phrase in Your Word today that "all your children will be taught by the Lord," I have new hope like a breath of fresh air. In Your great love and kindness, You included a promise directed at parents and specifically for our children. Lord, reveal how much more involved You are in my child's life than I have ever thought. Help me cling to this promise with both hands as my child has rejected my attempts to teach him a better way.

Lord, fulfill the role of teacher in my child. Assure my heart afresh, O Lord, that You are actively at work as You reach into the deep crevices of his heart and caverns of his soul. Lead him into the discovery that Your ways are best. Bring transformation to his spiritual condition as his darkened heart has brought disastrous effects on him physically and emotionally. I long for peace to be the experience and the atmosphere that my child comes to know.

Lord, teach me to be sensitive to Your Spirit, so I know what to do. And, meanwhile, increase my faith that You will teach my child.

I have fresh hope that together we will be learning that Your ways are life-releasing and speak of a preferred future.

In Jesus's name, amen.

DECREE

The Lord is my child's teacher. He will teach him, call him to repentance, and instruct him in the right way to live. God will teach him the proper path and draw him back even when he goes astray. As God teaches him, my child will declare the wondrous deeds of the Lord, and great will be his peace!

Psalm 25:8; Luke 5:32; Psalm 71:17

Day Ten

GOD IS A HEART-CHANGER

I will sprinkle clean water on you, and you will be clean; I will cleanse you from all your impurities and from all your idols. I will give you a new heart and put a new spirit in you; I will remove from you your heart of stone and give you a heart of flesh.
(Ezekiel 36:25-26)

MY PRAYER

FATHER, I STAND IN THE gap and intercede for my child, who has turned away from You and Your ways. Let my faith in You be greater than the difficulty of understanding what has happened in his life. Remove the cover of deception over his mind as he has turned from Your truths. Lift from me the deep pain of seeing him search in all the wrong ways for life's meaning and purpose. Guard my persuasion based on Your Word that all the peace he seeks is found in Your truth. Keep me attentive to Your Spirit's guidance and aware of Your work in his heart when I see how he struggles, and I do not know how to help him.

In my distress, I call upon You, Father, to help change his heart—even giving him a new heart that You have promised. Father, You have given me this child. He is in my family and is so very close to my heart. Because I am in Your family, Father, I call on You to soften his heart and turn it back to You, to our family, and to the family of God.

I remember the many times I saw glimpses of my child's destiny. I have not lost sight of that. I still believe that, with Your help, You will fulfill this destiny.

In Jesus's name, amen.

DECREE

I decree, by faith, that my child will be healed, delivered, set free, and changed by the power of God. I stand on the word of God that God is a heart-changer. You are creating a new heart within my child and displacing the lies and the damage. You are designing a new heart and putting a new spirit in him. All the days ordained for him have been written by the Lord. I stand on the scripture in agreement of this: As for me and my house, we will serve the Lord.

Psalm 107:20; Psalm 51:10; Psalm 139:16; Joshua 24:15

Day Eleven

GOD IS FAITHFUL

God is faithful, who has called you into
fellowship with his Son, Jesus Christ our Lord.
(1 Corinthians 1:9)

Let us hold unswervingly to the hope
we profess, for he who promised is faithful.
(Hebrews 10:23)

MY PRAYER

DEAR GOD, I HAVE KNOWn You to be faithful throughout my life. Today, I celebrate that You have been true to the promises in Your Word. Remind me afresh of the many ways You have demonstrated Yourself as father, rescuer, comforter, and provider. Stir to my memory the times when You impressed upon me that You had a plan and purpose for my child's life. Remind me how You often spoke that into my heart when he was but a baby and into his childhood. This was confirmed by men and women of God time and again over the years of his life.

Even though most days indicate that drugs are ruling his life, show me that You haven't set aside either Your promises or Your power to bring change. Renew my expectation, O Lord, that the outcome for our family will reflect Your promises. Forgive me for the many times I try to understand the reasons for the contradictions of my child's waywardness. Protect my heart, especially when his sinful choices produce disastrous results opposite to the promise of Your plans in his life.

When I do not recognize that You are at work, help me hold to the hope that my child will learn to discern what is best. Cause the worldly things that have enticed him to lose their appeal. Bring him the awareness that what the enemy has brought are distractions and entrapping snares. Contradict the enemy's lies. Show him that Your promises are true, and You remain faithful to them. Remove all distractions from his true calling. Grant that our entire household will once again celebrate You as our loving and faithful God.

In Jesus's name, amen.

DECREE

God is faithful in keeping His promises and His covenant of love. There is no end to His faithful love. Because of His great love and our love for Him, He will keep His promises to my family through-out a thousand generations. He is able and ready to strengthen both my child and me and protect us from the evil one. His compassions will never fail. In fact, they are new every morning. Great and abundant is His faithfulness!

Deuteronomy 7:9; 2 Thessalonians 3:3; Lamentations 3:22-23; Psalm 36:5

Day Twelve

GOD-GIVEN SPIRITUAL WEAPONS

For though we live in the world,
we do not wage war as the world does.
The weapons we fight with are not the weapons
of the world. On the contrary, they have divine
power to demolish strongholds. We demolish
arguments and every pretension that sets itself
up against the knowledge of God, and we take
captive every thought to make it obedient
to Christ. (2 Corinthians 10:3-5)

MY PRAYER

FATHER, I AM LEARNING IN my life and through Your Word that my family and I are in a battle. Teach me how to be victorious in this spiritual battle for my child's soul, mind, and body. As I am taught in Your Word, strengthen my grip on the weapons that have divine power to demolish strongholds. Thank You for giving me an effective tool against thoughts and beliefs that are contrary to Your truth. Fill me with Your divine power, so I can use my spiritual weapons to break down these strongholds.

My child has believed the enemy's lies about Your goodness, who You are, and Your plans for him. Do Your deep work, O Lord, and replace the lies with the truth that Your plans for him are for good and not for harm. Stir afresh that vision of Your desire for his life. Whenever the enemy attempts to extinguish hopeful expectations, give my child hope and a glimpse of a purpose-filled future.

And, for my part, O Lord, I reach to You for victorious thoughts toward Your ability to bring this to pass as I refuse the enemy's contradictory threats. Place a strong guard, O Lord, over my confident expectation that lies deep within me that indeed my child will come to freedom from his addiction, his rebellion, and all the enemy's lies.

In Jesus's name, amen.

DECREE

I have spiritual weapons to break down strongholds. The Word of God is the sword that I wield. Strongholds are demolished (torn down) in Jesus's name. Every pretension, speculation, and thought that sets itself up against the true knowledge of God in my child and myself is destroyed. Each thought is taken captive and made obedient to Christ. The stronghold of rebellion is broken in the name of Jesus Christ, including rebellion against all authority. God's plans are to prosper my child, giving him hope and the fulfillment of his future.

Ephesians 6:12, 17; Jeremiah 29:11

Day Thirteen

CHRIST, GIVER OF FREEDOM

*...If you hold to my teaching, you are really my
disciples. Then you will know the truth, and the
truth will set you free... So if the Son sets you free,
you will be free indeed.* (John 8:31-32, 36)

MY PRAYER

DEAR GOD, TODAY I AM seeking freedom for my child and me. As I look to You and Your Word, lead our household to Your truth that leads to freedom from sin and freedom from worry. Help me to hold Your teaching, so I will know the truth that will set me free. Many times, I have been immobilized by worry. Worry is the opposite of trusting You. I repent of worrying when I know You are active and at work. I thank You for the correction in Your Word that sets me free from worry. Remind me that I can live in an atmosphere of freedom as a sure thing because of You and Your Son, Jesus. Continue to search my heart, Lord, for any ways that I have failed to align with Your work as the Spirit of truth.

Thank You for the work of the cross and for setting my child and me free from the bondages that we have allowed through doubting and rejecting Your truth. Even as Your love was demonstrated on the cross for us, I ask that Your Spirit will now reveal to my child how deceptive the ways are that he has embraced. In Your mercy, show my child how destructive these choices are. Give me a refreshed expectation that he will be delivered and set free when the truth is revealed to him. Renew my stamina as I long for the deliverance and freedom provided by the cross to be the experience and testimony of my child.

In Jesus's name, amen.

DECREE

I will hold fast to the Lord's teaching and His words, "Do not worry." The truth has power to set my child and me free. Freedom from both sin and worry is ours because of Jesus's completed work on the cross. Because Jesus came to set captives free, we are free indeed. I proclaim freedom for my entire household!

Matthew 6:25-34; Galatians 5:1; Luke 4:18

Day Fourteen

JESUS IS THE LIGHT

*The god of this age has blinded the minds of
unbelievers, so that they cannot see the light of
the gospel that displays the glory of Christ, who is
the image of God.* (2 Corinthians 4:4)

*When Jesus spoke again to the people, he said,
"I am the light of the world. Whoever follows me
will never walk in darkness, but will have
the light of life."* (John 8:12)

MY PRAYER

DEAR GOD, EVEN THOUGH YOU are the only true source of light in
our world, there appears to be so much darkness. I see the darkness around my child where he is walking and spending his time. I
see that the enemy has blinded him to the truth of who You are and
is attempting to keep Your truth shrouded in darkness. Because of
this, he is not seeing or recognizing what is good for him.

Lord, remove the blindness over my child's mind that is block-
ing the light of the gospel that displays the glory of Christ, Your

Son. I ask, God, that You would cause Your light to shine in my child's heart and mind bringing revelation and understanding of the knowledge of Your glory. As You shine Your light in his life, I pray he would return to You and to the knowledge of all that is true and good. Cause my child to know Your love and compassion for him and for the world.

In Jesus's name, amen.

DECREE

My child will follow Jesus, the true Light of the world. He will not walk in the darkness. He will be one who is known to live as a child of the light. The fruit of light (goodness, righteousness, and truth) will become the expression of his life. He will discover what pleases God. God's Word within him is a lamp to his feet and a light to his path. The Lord will be his everlasting light, and the days of his sorrow will end. Hallelujah! The light has overcome the darkness! Jesus's light is life for my child and the light of all men!

Ephesians 5:8-10; Psalm 119:105; Isaiah 60:20; John 1:4-5

Day Fifteen

GOD IS OUR COMFORT

Praise be to the God and Father of our Lord Jesus
Christ, the Father of compassion and the God of
all comfort, who comforts us in all our troubles,
so that we can comfort those in any trouble with
the comfort we ourselves receive from God....
And our hope for you is firm, because we know
that just as you share in our sufferings, so also you
share in our comfort. (2 Corinthians 1:3-4, 7)

MY PRAYER

DEAR GOD, OUR FAMILY HAS been experiencing many troubles in this season. I find I am also grieving many losses as a mother. Receive this burden of the abundance of pain, despair, and anguish that has come. At times, it feels like it is beyond my ability to endure. Bring Your comfort to me, which is so needed in whatever way You so graciously choose. Already, I received Your comfort through Your Word, Your Spirit, and through Your people. I thank You for these as well as the comfort of Your promises. You are the wonderful, unfailing source of all that has been shared with me.

Lord, help me to hold onto You and Your Word in my weakness. Increase my understanding that You are the Father of compassion and the God of all comfort. Lord, guard my heart against all doubt that You would ever withhold comfort. This has often been the enemy's lie to me. I will, instead, receive the assurance that You comfort me, my child, and my family in our troubles. What a wonderful promise! Rekindle the flame of expectation that our family will indeed, against all odds, experience it.

Forgive me for the times I have harboured resentment toward You when I felt abandoned. Help me to settle my expectations and hope on You as my ultimate source of comfort. Lord, when I falter and fall back into anxiety, please remind me that You are a good, good God who knows the end from the beginning, and You are with us through it all.

I am so thankful today, God, for this comfort that You bring to me through others and even to others through me. I am humbled, and I never cease to marvel that You help me comfort others in their trouble.

In Jesus's name, amen.

DECREE

God is my comfort, my hope, and my salvation. He is compassionate and comforts me in all my troubles and grief. I am not afraid because God is with me. He will give me the strength and help I need with His hand as well as through other means. God sends comfort through his people. God will use me to comfort those in need with the comfort I have received from Him. Praise be to God! The comforter has come!

Isaiah 51:12; Isaiah 41:10; John 14:16

Day Sixteen

GOD WHO SEES MY HEART

My sacrifice, O God, is a broken spirit; a broken
and contrite heart you, God, will not despise.
(Psalm 51:17)

The Lord does not look at the things people look
at. People look at the outward appearance, but
the Lord looks at the heart. (1 Samuel 16:7)

MY PRAYER

LORD, TODAY I COME TO You in a broken state. My heart breaks for my child, who is struggling so much. I try to help, but he interprets my attempts as if I were coming against him. Lord, You see that my heart wants the best for my child even when he does not see it. The enemy deceives him into making claims and accusations against me that are not true. Thank You for helping me recognize that these accusations are not valid. Yet, Lord, You alone know how they have pierced my heart.

My eyes have been opened to see the source of these accusations. Therefore, the accuser no longer has power over me. False accusations may come at me through my child, but I now know they are from the enemy who wants me to feel defeated. I bring my heart before You, God. How thankful I am that You see my heart and know my intentions. You know the love I have for my child.

When I make a mistake or fail to take a step you may have intended for me to take, forgive me. Reveal to me afresh that You do not despise nor reject me. You graciously turn it for good. In Your goodness, You are teaching me many things as I walk out my faith.

Continue to shield and protect my heart. Thank You for showing me the truth. I ask You to continue to guide me as I have many difficult decisions to make as a parent, especially during this season.

In Jesus's name, amen.

DECREE

As a child of God, I am forgiven. I am appointed and anointed by God to be the mother of this child. God knows my heart. He is leading and guiding me into all truth. The enemy's lies and accusations are exposed and have lost their power. Having put on the full armour of God, today, I am taking a stand against his schemes. I have been set free!

1 John 2:12; John 16:13; Revelation 12:10; Ephesians 6:11;
Galatians 5:1

Day Seventeen

GOD IS MY CHILD'S PROTECTOR

*My prayer is not that you take them out of the
world but that you protect them from the evil one.
They are not of the world, even as I am not of it.
Sanctify them by the truth; your word is truth. As
you sent me into the world, I have sent them into
the world. For them I sanctify myself, that they too
may be truly sanctified.* (John 17:15-19)

*Whoever dwells in the shelter of the Most
High will rest in the shadow of the Almighty.*
(Psalm 91:1)

MY PRAYER

FATHER, MY CHILD NEEDS PROTECTION from the evil one. The
enemy is out to steal, kill, and destroy the destiny You have for
him. The evil one has been planting lies in his mind about You,
God, and about Your goodness. As a result, he believes these lies
and has become angry, turning away from You and all that is good
for him. He is on a path that is destroying his life and weakening
his physical body.

I pray that You protect him from the evil one, bringing Your truth and Your Word to his mind. Even let him have vivid memories of his earlier experiences of Your goodness. These will displace the contradictory lies of his enemy. As Jesus prayed for his disciples to be protected from the evil one, I pray this same protection for my child.

Thank you, Father, that You are our shelter. I step out of my agony and anxiety to find rest in Your shadow that is Your very presence. I ask that You bring Your presence of peace for today.

In Jesus's name, amen.

DECREE

I fear the Lord, and, in Him, I have a secure fortress. The Lord is a shelter for us to dwell in, and, in His shadow, we will find rest. His very presence provides protection. The Spirit of Truth guides us into all truth as a defence against our enemy. Our God is both a refuge and a strength. His ever-present help champions over fear. We are refreshed as we recognize that He dwells within us as His temple.

Psalm 36:7; Psalm 32:6-8; John 16:13; Psalm 46:1-4

Day Eighteen

GOD IS THE GIVER OF LIFE

The thief comes only to steal and kill and destroy;
I have come that they may have life, and have it
to the full. (John 10:10)

MY PRAYER

DEAR GOD, MY HEART BREAKS as I witness the pain in my child's life because of sin and rebellious choices. I bring before You my inadequacy of what to do as I see him losing hope. Help him receive the truth about Your love and care and Your desire to give him abundant life. In Your wisdom and ultimate love, move upon his life to cause him to once again embrace and value the biblical teaching he has had. Stir within him again the memories of when he felt Your presence and gave witness to knowing he was loved. In Your mercy, reveal Your goodness that he has tried so hard to deny.

He has turned away from You and has chosen a destructive lifestyle. The enemy has lied to him about the consequences and caused the outcomes to appear favourable. Open his eyes, Lord, to the true nature of the thief that he has allowed to enter his heart and life.

Protect my heart, O Lord, from pain as I watch this avoidable deterioration of his health and life. Cause me to hold fast to the truth that Your power and plan is the opposite of the evil one. Stir me and build my faith and expectation as I cling to the knowledge of what a godly lifestyle could mean for him. In Your great grace, work in our family for the sake of our future, according to what You have desired for all who follow You.

Father, I am encouraged as I align in prayer with Your heart. Strengthen my expectation that what we have lost as a family will once again be ours.

In Jesus's name, amen.

DECREE

The Lord will restore and bless my child and our family. The story of our family is not over. The Lord, Himself, is the author and finisher of our faith. The Lord has written our days in His book before one of them came to be. The Lord will complete what He has started and will do what He has promised. His restoration power will give us life to the full.

Hebrews 12:2 (NKJV); Psalm 139:16; Psalm 138:8 (NLT);
Deuteronomy 30:3

Day Nineteen

GOD GIVES HELP THROUGH OTHERS

He has delivered us from such a deadly peril,
and he will deliver us again. On him we have
set our hope that he will continue to deliver us,
as you help us by your prayers. Then many will
give thanks on our behalf for the gracious favor
granted us in answer to the prayers of many.
(2 Corinthians 1:10-11)

MY PRAYER

DEAR GOD, I CONTINUALLY THANK You for the many people that are praying for my child. I am often overwhelmed by the compassionate response of your people towards us. These faithful servants have graciously given me scriptures, prayers, and words of encouragement. These have been a great source of help.

By Your grace, fortify my faith that You will heal, deliver, and set my child free. I freely confess that I need hope and encouragement to sustain my confidence in a desired outcome that will align with Your heart. Guard me against turning away to my flesh when I begin to falter. Direct me instead to the timely help of others from whom I have received fresh words, scriptures, or prayers. Without fail, these lift me from all counterfeit dependency. When I am tempted to feel alone in the battle, remind me that I am not alone.

Remind me again and again, Lord, to turn from looking at the bleak circumstances and focus instead on You and Your promises. Tell me again, even in my lowest moments, that deadly peril is not the end of our story. Your gracious favour and powerful deliverance will result in many giving thanks to Your great Name.

In Jesus's name, amen.

DECREE

We have confidence that the Lord hears our prayers and petitions and will answer. He is merciful and gives grace to help in our time of need. Encouragement will continue to come from our God. My child will receive gracious favour in answer to the prayers of many. God is faithful and will accomplish His purpose.

I John 5:14-15; Hebrews 4:16; 2 Thessalonians 2:16-17;
2 Thessalonians 1:11

Day Twenty

GOD GIVES INSTRUCTIONS FOR LIFE

My son, do not let wisdom and understanding out of your sight, preserve sound judgment and discretion; they will be life for you, an ornament to grace your neck. Then you will go on your way in safety, and your foot will not stumble. When you lie down, you will not be afraid; when you lie down your sleep will be sweet. (Proverbs 3:21-24)

MY PRAYER

O DEAR GOD, I HAVE done my best to diligently teach my child what is right and what is good, according to Your Word. Over these past few years, he has strayed from this teaching. In Your mercy, protect him, even though he chooses to wander from You and Your ways. I sense the resulting restlessness and frustration as he fills his nights and days with mind-numbing drugs. Do not turn Your eyes from him. Do not abandon him to the danger which he willingly has stepped. I long for him to see the beauty in living a godly life. Open my child's heart and mind to make a new commitment to Your ways. So much benefit awaits him in making that choice. Lead him again to the way of safety. Open his heart to Your instructions.

Set his foot back into Your path when he stumbles. Peace in the daytime and through the dark nights awaits him. Stir to my child's remembrance the teachings from Your Word and the goodness they offer. May they have more attraction than the ways of the world that lead to destruction and death.

When I see the disastrous results of these choices, please protect me and my faith. Help me to use wisdom, sound judgment, and discretion. I am grateful for how often You remind me that Your ways are right and good. Refresh my expectation of how Your ways will direct my child.

In Jesus's name, amen.

DECREE

Surely my child will see the goodness of God in the land of the living. He will delight in the Lord who makes his steps firm. He will follow the path of righteousness where there is life. He will be diligent in choosing righteousness and in practicing these things so that he will not stumble.

Psalm 27:13; Psalm 37:23; Proverbs 12:28; 2 Peter 1:10

Day Twenty-One

GOD IS OUR HELPER

So do not fear, for I am with you; do not be dismayed, for I am your God. I will strengthen you and help you; I will uphold you with my righteous right hand... For I am the Lord your God who takes hold of your right hand and says to you, Do not fear; I will help you. (Isaiah 41:10, 13)

MY PRAYER

DEAR GOD, AS I READ Your Words in Isaiah 41, I am becoming more certain You understand my feelings and concerns for my child. I ask for Your help to maintain this certainty. Help me with the fear and dismay I have felt over many things in the chaotic swirl created by addictions. Take hold of my hand, O Lord, when I am overcome with a sense of helplessness as to how to shield him. Reveal Your willingness and readiness to be our help when I am fearful for my child's life and his safety. I am beyond my own ability. Help me let go of my fear and lay hold of Your promise. Show me again, Lord, that because I belong to You, I am assured that I will find my strength in You.

Lord, please also help my child. I pray that You would give him strength and hold him up when he cannot hold himself up. God, I know when I call on You, You will respond in diligent care to help us. Thank You for reassuring me in Your Word that You are with me and that You are my God. When I fear You have left us alone in this place of uncertainty, help me to remember that You will never leave us. By Your grace, empower me to consistently proclaim that You will not abandon my child or me. Today, I am confident that I am upheld by the strength and strong grip of Your right hand.

In Jesus's name, amen.

DECREE

I will not fear. The Lord is the stronghold of my life. He is mindful of us in our present state. He watches over us, keeping us from harm and watching over our lives. He will not abandon us. He is faithful to His Word, promising to help, deliver, and love. This promise is continual, and He will not delay.

Psalm 27:1; Psalm 121:1-8; Psalm 40:17

Day Twenty-Two

GOD IS OUR RESCUER

"Because he loves me," says the Lord, "I will rescue him; I will protect him, for he acknowledges my name. He will call on me, and I will answer him; I will be with him in trouble, I will deliver him and honor him." (Psalm 91:14-15)

MY PRAYER

DEAR GOD, THERE IS SO much that is not looking good for my child at this time. There has been a progression of increased trouble as he has turned away from You. He has turned to drugs, then to crime, and is now facing the consequences. When I read the scripture today in Psalm 91, I can envision my child acknowledging Your name and calling on You. Remind me that You are there with him in his trouble to protect him, rescue him, deliver him, and honour him. How I long to see the fulfillment of this in his life!

Even now, in his self-chosen difficulties, awaken my child's heart to see the truth of Your promise in Psalm 91. Restore to him a clear picture of what You desire life to be for him. Let him now turn and look to You as a source of help. Lord, help me to take my focus off the present circumstances and to thank You for today. Give me fresh faith for what You are doing in the hidden places of my child's heart. Awaken new expectations that the promise of Your future for my child will be realized. Graciously, You have confirmed Your intentions to me numerous times through Your Word. I thank You that this renewed focus will strengthen me for today.

In Jesus's name, amen.

DECREE

The Lord will rescue, protect, and bring deliverance to my child. He will be rescued from the dominion of darkness and brought into the kingdom of the Son. The Lord will show my child His salvation and satisfy him with long life. According to the promise in God's Word, as I believe, I anticipate that my household will also be saved.

Colossians 1:13-14; Psalm 91:16; Acts 16:31

Day Twenty-Three

GOD'S LIFE-RESTORING POWER

He asked me, "Son of man, can these bones live?"
I said, "Sovereign Lord, you alone know." Then he
said to me, "Prophesy to these bones and say to
them, '"Dry bones, hear the word of the Lord! This
is what the Sovereign Lord says to these bones: I
will make breath enter you, and you will
come to life.'" (Ezekiel 37:3-5)

MY PRAYER

FATHER, I STAND IN AWE at the way You hold all power and that You work "against all odds." As I read the picture You showed Your servant, Ezekiel, it lifted me again from the hopelessness that I am prone to fall prey to. All around me, I see that our life has been replaced with ruins. It seems that our address has been the graveyard of dreams I have carried for my child. Please, Lord, remind me of Your life-restoring power. When I see my son's life as a dry, parched land of discouragement, anger, deception, pain, and suffering, create the life of vitality and excitement of youth again.

Restore to me those earlier dreams and visions You gave me for my family. Help me recognize that You are still at work breathing

Your breath into them, even when I see the opposite. Thank you that You overcome and are the answer to impossible circumstances.

In Jesus's name, amen.

DECREE

The Lord gives life and calls things that are not as though they were. I believe and will speak of the Lord's power to restore life with the same spirit of faith. He brings beauty out of ashes. I will not despair. I believe the Lord can and will move our mountain of need. He has power to do what He has said He will do concerning my child and his destiny. I believe I will receive what I have asked for in prayer for my child and his future.

Romans 4:17; 2 Corinthians 4:13; Isaiah 61:3; Mark 11:22-24

Day Twenty-Four

JESUS IS OUR EXAMPLE

*... fixing our eyes on Jesus, the pioneer and
perfecter of faith. For the joy set before him he
endured the cross, scorning its shame, and sat
down at the right hand of the throne of God.
Consider him who endured such opposition from
sinners, so that you will not grow weary
and lose heart.* (Hebrews 12:2-5)

MY PRAYER

DEAR GOD, YOUR SON, JESUS, endured much for us through the work of the cross from start to finish. Jesus understands opposition and struggles. This is such an encouragement to know that You and Your Son understand how I feel. Help me, Lord, to keep my eyes fixed on Your Son and the accomplishments of the cross. Your Son is the perfect example of living, serving, suffering, forgiving, loving, and staying in a close relationship with You. The cross made a way for our salvation, healing, and deliverance. And the cross opened the way to a close relationship with You. Help me to remember this, so I will not grow weary or lose heart.

Today, release Your grace upon me to look past the circumstances that are swirling around our home because of the destructive choices my child has made. As I choose to set my eyes instead on You and Your ways, lift off of me the paralyzing weariness. Help me to continue to find strength in You. Draw me again and again into Your Word so that I am reminded where to place my focus and thus endure hardships. Lord, as You help me to fix my eyes on Jesus, Your Son, also help me to follow His example as the pioneer and perfector of faith.

In Jesus's name, amen.

DECREE

Today I fix my eyes on Jesus and not my circumstances. I will not grow weary and lose heart. I will find strength as my eyes are on Jesus. He will work miracles beyond what I could ask or imagine (immeasurably more). I will rejoice and be glad in Him, saying, "The Lord is great." He is mountain-moving, and He makes the impossible possible. In both His deeds and His Word, He encourages my heart and strengthens me.

Ephesians 3:20-21; Matthew 19:26; 2 Thessalonians 2:16-17; Psalm 40:16

Day Twenty-Five

GOD GRANTS FAVOUR

May the favor of the Lord our God rest on us;
establish the work of our hands for us—yes,
establish the work of our hands. (Psalm 90:17)

MY PRAYER

FATHER, I HAVE COME BEFORE You many times in need of comfort and reassurance. As I read Your Word today, I read of the psalmist's request for Your favour. That is now my cry for our household. Let us come under the influence of Your divine kindness and compassion. We seek Your blessing. Thank You that Your favour is available to me as Your follower. I ask You for the continued expressions of Your love towards my family and me. Our need is great, and we require supernatural favour.

Open my heart to have confidence that Your favour includes Your power to produce change. I thank You in advance that You can redirect the course of my child's life back to the path You have chosen for him. Lord, establish the work of our hands by Your mighty hand.

And I pray for Your power to continue to work in my life as I attempt to diligently fill so many roles: Your servant, a daughter, a labourer, a coworker, a friend, and a parent. I call upon Your divine guidance and favour in the many decisions to be made, particularly those regarding my child. I present to You the daily demands of these tasks in each of these roles of my life. Lord, so many times, I have questioned my actions and have doubted the decisions I made. Forgive me for trying to do this on my own. In Your grace, remind me that I can ask and trust You. Bless and establish the work of my hands for Your eternal good and glory.

In Jesus's name, amen.

DECREE

The Lord has saved us by His grace. It is His power that changes things for us! He bestows favour on us in His kindness for His eternal purposes. My hope is in the Lord. His favour brings evidence of His goodness and mercy working in our lives.

Ephesians 2:8; Ephesians 3:10-11; Zechariah 4:6; Luke 1:25, 50

Day Twenty-Six

GOD IS WITH ME

...This is what the LORD says to you:
"Do not be afraid or discouraged because of this
vast army. For the battle is not yours, but God's....
You will not have to fight this battle. Take up your
positions; stand firm and see the deliverance the
Lord will give you, Judah and Jerusalem.
Do not be afraid; do not be discouraged. Go out
to face them tomorrow, and the Lord will be
with you." (2 Chronicles 20:15, 17)

MY PRAYER

DEAR FATHER, I CONFESS THAT I have been afraid and discouraged by the increase of trouble that has come since sin and addiction have entered my family's territory. I have spent countless sleepless nights and pain-filled days trying to figure out a way to get through it. Yet, Lord, Your Word assures me that I am not alone and that the battle is Yours. Help me to take hold of this reality. When I am afraid or discouraged by the trouble I see, help me to take a position of faith and prayer. Help me to stand firm in faith to see what You will do on behalf of my child and our family.

I acknowledge how involved You are in my family. I am humbled and in awe. Remind me again of those many times when there has been evidence of Your work in our midst. Many things have turned out for good that initially did not appear to be resulting in our favour. Yet, by a miraculous turn of events, there were victorious outcomes. I give You the glory, Lord! Forgive me, Lord, for relying on my own understanding and not trusting You in everything. I choose to face my tomorrows with faith and confidence in You.

In Jesus's name, amen.

DECREE

I have victory through my Lord, Jesus Christ! No longer will I be moved from what is His desire to give us as our inheritance. He has pledged to be with us and watch over us always. We will never be abandoned by His care. He is faithfully demonstrating His desire and ability to fulfill everything promised. I am standing firm and holding my position to see the salvation of the Lord! My help comes from the Lord who made heaven and earth! The Lord is and will be with me!

I Corinthians 15:57; Genesis 28:15; Psalm 121:1-2

Day Twenty-Seven

GOD IS LOVING, PATIENT, AND KIND

*The Lord is not slow in keeping his promise, as
some understand slowness. Instead he is patient
with you, not wanting anyone to perish, but
everyone to come to repentance.* (2 Peter 3:9)

MY PRAYER

FATHER, I UNDERSTAND FROM YOUR Word that You are not slow in keeping Your promise. Refresh my faith in Your timing, Lord. Ours has been a long and difficult journey without the manifestation of the anticipated outcome. At times, these present circumstances in our family appear to be contradictory to Your promise. There are many things I do not yet understand. Open my eyes to align with Your patience and Your compassion, which have never been withdrawn from us.

Lord, forgive me for not always using Your Word as my lens to understand Your ways. I submit afresh to Your timing. Help me also to have the patience to endure until the desired outcome: the freedom and salvation of my child. Let me embrace what seems like a delay to be an expression of Your kindness to us.

Your desire is for everyone, including my family, to come to repentance. Help me keep this truth paramount in my mind, especially when I am trying to make sense of things. I thank You for Your patience with my child and me. I am sure that You are and will continue to work in our hearts and lives, bringing the fullness of Your promise to us.

In Jesus's name, amen.

DECREE

The Lord is gracious, compassionate, slow to anger, and abounding in steadfast love. He is continually at work bringing salvation to my family. My hope is in Him. I will seek Him and wait quietly for His salvation. His kindness leads to repentance. My child will come to repentance. In God's timing, he will turn from his ways and return to the Lord and live. This will be pleasing to the Lord.

Joel 2:13; Lamentations 3:25-26; Romans 2:4;
Ecclesiastes 3:1; Ezekiel 18:23

Day Twenty-Eight

GOD BLESSES US AS PEACEMAKERS

*Blessed are the peacemakers, for they will be
called children of God.* (Matthew 5:9)

MY PRAYER

DEAR GOD, WITH YOUR HELP and by Your Spirit, I desire to be a peacemaker in my family. The challenge arises regularly. Often, I find myself in conflict with my child. This is not a place I desire to be. I find it difficult when the conflict comes from his rebellion. I find myself longing for those former times when peace, love, and joy were present in our home. Turn my disappointment into an opportunity to show godliness when I see how much he has turned from what he has been taught. Replace our opposing positions with Your grace, mercy, and truth.

Lord, I ask that You bring reconciliation and restore peace in my family. And, as I trust You and eagerly anticipate the transformation, help me to be an instrument of Your peace. I especially need You to help me when the conflict increases and emotions are hot. Send swift awareness and conviction when I respond with accusation. In those hard times, I need Your grace and mercy working within me to give me wisdom and compassion. I pray You would quiet my frustration at the turn of events. I ask for Your peace to replace my discontent. Thank You, Lord, for Your presence and Your active work in my family and me.

In Jesus's name, amen.

DECREE

The Lord is my help and salvation to my family and me. I am being graced to be a peacemaker to minister the reconciliation of my family to God through Christ. I will be blessed, reaping a harvest of righteousness. Now is the time of God's favour and the day of salvation for us. I will rejoice!

2 Corinthians 5:18; James 3:18; 2 Corinthians 6:2; Philippians 4:4

Day Twenty-Nine

GOD WORKS IN ALL THINGS FOR GOOD

*And we know that in all things God works for
the good of those who love him, who have been
called according to his purpose.... If God is for us,
who can be against us?* (Romans 8:28, 31)

MY PRAYER

DEAR GOD, YOU HAVE SHOWN Yourself faithful in miraculous ways.
When I begin to doubt, remind me again of how You have vigilantly
watched over my child and kept him alive. Build my faith again as
I realize how many of the details of our lives You are involved in,
even when I am so mired down in need. When it seems like we are
losing the battle, remind me that you continue to work in all things
for the good of those who love You. Keep my expectation steadfast
for my child's freedom from addiction. In my hour of need, bring
Your words and promises to keep my faith strong amid the abundance of unexpected and chaotic events.

Lord, continue to work in my child's life. I look to You, especially when my numerous attempts at sorting it all out and giving
sound advice seem futile. Be my wisdom when I frequently face
the decision whether to step in and be involved or to step back and

wait. Help me to trust You for Your continued intervention. Let me take comfort in the assurance that You are at work. You work for the good of those who love You. I am thankful You are for us and are intricately involved in our lives, working things "for the good!"

In Jesus's name, amen.

DECREE

God's intentions for my child are for good. He is at work to save his life. Our God is the God of "all grace." The Lord will restore us and make us strong, firm, and steadfast. All things are possible to those who believe. He will help our unbelief and will continue to work miracles on our behalf.

Genesis 50:20; 1 Peter 5:10; Mark 9:23-25

Day Thirty

REJOICING COMES IN THE MORNING!

*For his anger lasts only a moment, but his favor
lasts a lifetime; weeping may stay for the night,
but rejoicing comes in the morning.* (Psalm 30:5)

*I remain confident of this: I will see the goodness
of the Lord in the land of the living.* (Psalm 27:13)

MY PRAYER

DEAR FATHER, THERE HAVE BEEN so many hours, days, and months
of weeping. I felt like the psalmist who described that he would
have despaired had he not believed he would see the goodness of
God in the land of the living. This belief and the support of others
who also believed helped to sustain me.

I am rejoicing, now, as I see the manifestation of Your promises. Through a turn of events that could have led to further darkness and despair, I have seen my child turn to You, Lord, and Your
Word. He sees You now as a source of help and Your way as the
way he should walk. He is now reading Your Word, holding onto
Your teaching, and choosing Your path of life. Help him, Lord, to

continue this path of righteousness and continued freedom. Help me to gently guide him and not hinder him.

Lord, Your favour truly lasts a lifetime. Help us both as we navigate the road that leads us forward in recovery and freedom. May Your love be the glue that holds us together as a family and bonds us to You. Help me not to waver in my expectation that the change will surely continue despite growing pains or convoluted paths. Even these, with Your continued intervention, will still lead forward. Help me to remember that although there may yet be times of weeping, Your promise is that joy comes in the morning.

In Jesus's name, amen.

DECREE

Blessing and joy have come to my household! Before, I had seen the Lord accomplish supernatural work only in other lives and families. Now, my eyes have seen that demonstration up close! God is faithful and good. His anger lasts only for a moment, but His favour lasts for a lifetime. Weeping may stay for the night, but rejoicing comes in the morning! He has turned my mourning into (joyful) dancing and clothes me with joy. My heart will sing His praises and not be silent. I will Praise Him forever!

Job 42:5; Psalm 27:13 (AMP); Psalm 30:5, 11-12 (NLT)

Part Two

A Letter from My Son

Because You Prayed

THANK YOU FROM JUSTIN

THANK YOU, MOM—BECAUSE YOU PRAYED

I WANT TO SAY SOMETHING to you, Mom, for the prayers that you prayed for me. I know that they started before I was even born and continue to this day. I can feel them lift me up and surround me every day, and I have learned to rely on them. Just knowing that you are praying gives me relief and peace, no matter what I am going through.

Those prayers helped me in my darkest nights, even when I didn't know it. I can see it now that there is no greater force than a praying mother and no greater help to a lost boy. I know it must have been hard for you, seeing Your son go down the dark path of addiction. I know it hurt you to watch me hurt myself, but I know you never lost sight of what you knew was my destiny.

I don't know if what I want to say is an adequate response to the declarations you made over me, the sleepless nights and long days. Two words can never be enough to repay you for never giving up on me. But I want to say something to you because when my addiction seemed to take *everything* away from me, it never took my life, and it never took my destiny.

I can remember coming close to death and even wanting to die. I remember you standing over me in the hospital room and constantly praying. You held on for me, knowing that this wasn't going to be where I would be staying. I remember you watching over me in the courtroom, interceding and longing to see me make my way out and my way home. Even though I was pushing you away, and even though I despised Your help and took advantage of you, you never stopped praying.

I know today that your prayers not only rescued me from the grip of death, but they carried me into my destiny. I'm sure you know Eph 3:20, where it says that He is able to do abundantly more than we could ever ask or imagine. Well, today, it feels like I am living in that verse! Because of your prayers, I was able to realize that I was created to bring glory to God and not only to be successful in life but also to be successful in the call that God had on my life. Your prayers paved the way for me to step into my ministry so that I could begin to help those like me find the same hope that I found.

And finally, your prayers did something that I never expected and didn't even know was possible. Your prayers helped me become the man I am today, the man who was able to get married to an amazing girl and become the father of three amazing children.

This is what you knew was true even though I didn't realize it. Your declarations over me and hopes for me have become my reality. Because you prayed, I didn't just get rescued from death. I realized my destiny.

What I want to say may seem so small in comparison, but with all these things in my mind and with all my heart, I want to *thank you* for praying for me. Thank you for fighting for me and for lifting me up time and time again. Thank you for your unwavering faith and unconditional love. Thank you for declaring truth in the midst of the lies. Thank you.

I know many children are in similar situations, and many other mothers are making declarations over them. My prayer is that this book helps those in the midst of the battle, that they would be assured that they aren't alone in the struggle and that they won't be alone in the victory.

So, to you reading this book, who are fervently praying on behalf of your son or daughter (even though they can't say it right now), thank *you* for your prayers. They are riding on your love like a lifeboat, longing to come home. I am confident of this, that one day soon they will thank you themselves, as your declarations become their reality.

In confident expectation,
Your son,
Justin

CONCLUSION

EVEN THOUGH DIFFICULT TIMES STILL come, I keep learning to trust in God and His Word. I still believe that prayers from a mother's heart for her children are precious to God, and not one of them goes unheard. Each day, I still put my son in God's loving hands. God has remained faithful.

During the writing of this book, when it was in its final stages, my third grandchild was born. I have once again seen the goodness of God in the land of the living. I am amazed and in awe that God has once again done abundantly more than I could think, ask, or imagine.

To you, the readers, I pray this resource will assist you as you seek God in prayer and the scriptures for hope, for strength, and for healing.

Shout for joy to God, all the earth!
Sing the glory of his name;
make his praise glorious.
Say to God, "How awesome are your deeds!
So great is Your power that your enemies
cringe before you.
All the earth bows down to you; they sing praise
to you, they sing the praises of your name.
Come and see what God has done...
(Psalm 66: 1-5)

Lightning Source UK Ltd.
Milton Keynes UK
UKHW021258060422
401177UK00011B/689

9 781486 622399